# The Common Traits Of Millionaires

## What They Have That You Don't

STEFAN CAIN

This page intentionally left blank.

# CONTENTS

# INTRODUCTION

> Marita: "John, we need a larger, more respectable office."
> John: "We can't afford it."
> Marita: "John, we have a million dollars!"
> John: "*Gasp!* We do?"

**True Story:**
John F. was just a salesman in the food industry, but he was a good one. He dreamed of moving into the upper management in his company. He was very hard-working, invested wisely, and saved his money. He was hoping to be wealthy in the future. One day – much to his surprise – he discovered he was a millionaire, as you can see in the above conversation. His story will appear in this book.

Can you too become a millionaire?

Yes, you can. Absolutely.

How?

1.  By following the "Half-Robin-Hood" principle: "Take from the rich and... keep it." (!!!)

2.  By enhancing your own current traits, and incorporating more of the millionaire traits into your own mindset. Those traits are typical traits that many people have – nothing spectacular. Millionaires have learned how to use them to their own advantage.

3.  By adopting the personality styles of millionaires. Most of us

already have some of those personality characteristics.

4.  By taking on a millionaire-minded monetary lifestyle and growing the capital to start your business, or climb up the corporate ladder in the company for which you now work.

5.  By identifying your most promising area of profitability – your niche.

6.  By developing a business plan and support systems.

This book will explore techniques # 2, 3, 4, 5, and 6. You wouldn't be pleased with the first method. Bernie Madoff at the Butner Federal Prison used that method. His ego got greater than his common sense.

Also covered will be the tax advantages you can have by developing a sole proprietorship, an LLC, or a Chapter S Corporation. General instructions for their formations will be discussed. Foreign entities also qualify for LLCs in the US, and – that way – they could broaden their customer base.

# 1

## THE COMMON TRAITS
## OF MILLIONAIRES

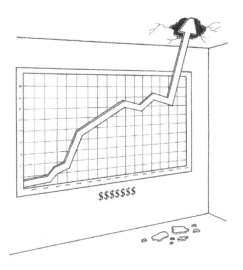

$$$$$$$

You may not have all the traits and personality factors present in most millionaires, but you have some of them. It is not essential that you develop ALL of them. Let's face it, millionaires are also human. They have more money than you do, but do not live on pedestals unless you build them. They are people. Some are eccentric; and some are slightly irascible. Those are shortcomings. They recognize that, and have learned how to compensate for those shortcomings as best they can. Here, you will read about the common traits of millionaires, and some of the recommendations about how you can enhance your strengths and compensate for your weaknesses. Your shortcomings may always be with you, but you can learn how to correct them – just like the millionaires have.

# The First and Greatest Trait:
## They Are Happy with Their Work

The multimillionaire, Warren Buffett, said: "I get to do what I like to do every single day of the year." He wasn't talking about fun in the sun; he was talking about his work. He wasn't talking about his money either; he was talking about how much he enjoys the daily challenge of working as a financier. He likes the excitement of it. Buffett has had his ups and downs like so many other millionaires, but he loves investing. He loves his work, and says he never wants to retire.

## Trust in Themselves

Some call for you to "Believe in Yourself," but that expression limps from its own ambiguity. If you want to believe in something, believe that you can be rich, but only if you so choose.

Within the mind of a millionaire lies an undying trust in himself. The millionaire trusts in his or her own judgement. Teasing and laughter from armchair critics goes unheeded. Millionaires do not make a flurry of phone calls to family and friends telling them of their intentions. Likewise, they do not consult with them. Their power comes from themselves and their carefully constructed business support systems.

# MARK ZUCKERBERG

Zuckerberg is most famous for being the founder of Facebook, which is a flourishing social media site. He started it in his college dormitory.

In the beginning, he was sometimes ridiculed for turning the internet into a place for play and gamers. Nevertheless, he pushed forward, recognizing the need for people to have a place for social contact. He believed in what he was doing. Recognizing the trends and peoples' desires for interaction, he knew he could win out in a very big way if he promoted this interactive concept. To pursue his quest, he reached out to other countries as well, trusting that the concept could make him a fortune. He knew he was underfunded, so he sought out the interest of those who could be convinced to finance his venture. As early as 2004, he also realized the potential for advertising revenue from Facebook, and knew he could increase his earnings substantially. He trusted wholeheartedly in himself.

## They Know How to Win Even if Times Get Tough

Not all millionaires were born rich. Everyone, even the poorest of people, have the ability to transform themselves, because that stems from the basic need to survive. Adaptability is the key to basic survival. In the beginning, models, dancers, and actors had to live in squalid conditions – five to a room in a cheap hotel – as they went from audition to audition in unfriendly areas of New York City and Hollywood. When they ran out of food, they donned their best clothes and supped for free at the public art openings. They changed their clothes in train station bathrooms when they had to go to auditions uptown. They were friendly with others in the business, and stopped by to take their showers at their apartments in the city. Sometimes, they were lucky and were invited to parties in the theater district. There was always plenty there to eat and drink.

As you read the synopses of some of the biographies in the discussion of the common traits of millionaires, you will note how many of them had very humble beginnings. There were many times they failed at achieving specific goals. The more that happened, the more they got used to it. In time their fears of failure decreased. You see, the realm of failure was no longer outside their comfort zone. They were there before, and knew they would survive.

One of the movies that Oprah Winfrey starred in, called *Native Son*, received very poor reviews. However, Oprah came from a humble background, and that didn't stop her from performing. A failure does not destroy an entire career. You too can survive failure.

If you know what it's like to be poor sometimes, you will be able to relate to many other people who are poor now. You can more easily understand your future customers who may be poor. Because of your experiences, you can market some of your products or services in such a way that the less fortunate can afford and benefit from them.

Knowledge about the poorer segment of society has given rise to huge discount stores and chains. Hence, you have stores like Walmart and a whole network of dollar stores. Stores and businesses that serve customers from all income levels do extremely well. It is a win-win situation for both the owners and the customers.

# OPRAH WINFREY

Oprah grew up on a very poor farm in rural Mississippi. When she was six years old, she was sent up north and lived in a very dangerous Milwaukee neighborhood. Oprah always dreamed about becoming a singer and entertainer.

Her mother worked several jobs and couldn't give Oprah the supervision and protection she needed. As result, she was sexually abused from the age of nine until she was in her teens. Later on, her mother sent her to Nashville to live with her father, hoping life would be better for her daughter.

During the time she spent with her father, Oprah never let go of her interest to become a public entertainer. Under her father's advice and discipline, she was able to develop her intellect and secured work as an anchor at a news station when she was only nineteen years old. Later on, she moved into the daytime talk show format, hosted the *Oprah Winfrey Show,* and later sponsored projects aimed at self-improvement and self-help.

## They Are Resilient

This is reminiscent of the quote "I'm back!" uttered by Jack Nicholson in his movie *The Shining.* Millionaires have learned resiliency after failures. They always bounce back because they are determined to be successful. No matter how far you tumble, if you are resilient, you do come back.

# JACK MA

Jack Ma is the founder of Alibaba, the internet business marketing technology company. It serves as a conduit for e-commerce and information platforms. In 2014, it secured a revered status on the stock market after its initial public offering.

As a young man, Jack Ma flunked many exams. In China, there are entry qualification exams given at different levels. Ma failed his entry exams for middle school on three occasions, and was rejected by Harvard University ten times. When he applied to work at Kentucky Fried Chicken, twenty-three candidates were selected from a pool of 24 – Jack was the only one turned down.

He was not a technological genius. It wasn't until he was 33-years-old that he even owned a computer. Jack Ma was an "idea" man, who recognized the fact that he needed others to compensate for what he lacked in skill. Due to his experiences in failure, he sought out investors and software specialists to aid in his undying quest. Jack knew that his genius lay in seeing a need and assessing a trend. That trend was the incredible power of the internet as a viable tool in business.

If you truly, truly want to be a millionaire someday like Jack Ma, even large setbacks and pitfalls will not stop your progress forward. While you may alter your approach or modify your original strategy, you will want to bounce back and move toward your ultimate goal. Every setback is not a failure; it is a learning experience. Even if it is an experience in how to fail, it has value. Once a failure is experienced, it becomes familiar and will be easier to handle if it happens again. No matter what, you will not stop trying. If you are adaptable and willing to take a different tactic, you will not fail.

# Delay of Gratification

Even if you don't make a million when you are just starting out, there is no reason why you can't make several hundred thousand dollars in a relatively short period of time, and increase your wealth. Money is a great motivator, but you may have to work very hard to have a lot of it.

If you don't make your first million in five years, experience and business connections increase as you age. Those are all stepping stones. Wise investing is essential. Even the most stable of professional fields and businesses go through low periods. Some even go bankrupt. However, companies can even come back, even from bankruptcy. They can do that through financial reorganization and the implanting of new ideas and new business approaches.

You will succeed, but perhaps not right this minute. Time is a blessing and you have a lifetime of supply.

One has to nurture a sense of delaying one's wish for gratification, especially of the monetary kind. Long-term planning is best. It is far better to hold off and wait for a greater reward later on. This takes a high degree of cognition, not to mention patience. Rushing too fast can do a lot of damage, such as that experienced by Samsung with their exploding phones.

A person needs to exercise self-control and willpower in order to become a millionaire. The impatient and impulsive lose out. Emotional centers in the brain are part of what is called the limbic system. Emotions tend to run wild depending on the information that enters through the senses. Only the higher brain functions can control them. The prefrontal cortex (the "thinking part" of your brain) analyzes possible choices and intercedes to initiate or impede a desired act. The delay of gratification is a cognitive affair.

# JOHN F.

John was the "star" of this book's introduction. You won't find his name in Wikipedia. He isn't interested in fame. John is just a hard-working guy who happens to make over a million dollars a year. You haven't heard of him. However, have you ever heard of *Saucy Susan?* Have you ever heard of taco seasoning? How about guacamole? John started out as the first salesman from his company to sell *Saucy Susan* and other Mexican spice products to the USA. He thought someday he might become the VP or perhaps the CEO of the company.

John always saved his money and invested it wisely. Initially, he intended that it would be used for a very pleasant retirement.

However, problems occurred in his company. Profits were declining and the management was growing weaker in its marketing approach. John was an excellent salesman who believed in the products. In an effort to keep the company afloat, he agreed to forego part of his salary temporarily, hoping that they would recover. Unfortunately, that didn't happen and his company was going to go out of business. They wanted to pay John his back salary, but didn't have have enough money. So John indicated that he would accept ownership of *Saucy Susan*, and a number of other products, in lieu of his back wages. Rather than look for other employment, he felt he could do something with the product. So he lived on his savings, determined that he would have the chance to make his money later on.

Because he was on a shoestring budget, he rented a small office in a lower socioeconomic area from a friend. That's where he mixed his spices. His friend still tells stories about how the whole building reeked of spices all day, every day. John mixed them, then hired a few helpers so he could reopen some distribution channels at grocery stores. John traveled back and forth to Mexico frequently to negotiate various deals. *Saucy Susan* and his other products sold extremely well in the US. He expanded and expanded until his Mexican products were nationally distributed. His company was now worth a fortune. He was willing to work hard and delay gratification until such time that he could sell his spice business and use some of that as seed money for a new pursuit. So he sold his *Saucy Susan* line and made a fortune.

John had a variety of interests, and wanted to move into commercial real estate. He became extremely wealthy in that venture as well and today owns many commercial buildings in the northeastern US. He married later in life, as do many millionaires. It is no surprise that John's lovely wife is Mexican.

## Inventiveness and Curiosity; Openness to Experience

The curious and inventive person engages and has engaged in a wide range of activities, sometimes just for sheer experience of exhilaration. Before making their fortunes, millionaires did not abide by a strict routine, but they made sure they got the basics of their lives taken care of.

Creativity of expression and a fondness for novelty describes them well. Intellectual curiosity is an ever-present feature of their personality. They often sit in their offices and muse to themselves: "What if…"

Elon Musk is an excellent example of this curiosity and openness to new experiences.

# ELON MUSK

Musk taught himself computer programming initially. He liked to create computer games. When he perfected one of his video games, he sold all the rights to it for only $500. That is well below market rates, because the buyers would be able to license hundreds of copies of the game to customers.

Elon's later attempts in his software business went well, but he was unable to become CEO of the company because of differences with his Board of Directors. He was undaunted in his pursuit of wealth and fervently sought an outlet for his curiosity. After he sold his shares in the company that he and his brother created, he realized that America had a need for less expensive rockets. Musk was very imaginative and open to new and unusual experiences. He had a personal interest in private space exploration, and tried to recruit the support and help of Russian designers. However, the Russians felt he was weak in his technical skills and wouldn't work with him. On his departure from there, he got a new idea, and decided that he could promote and build a less expensive rocket for the USA. That would fill the need for more efficient travel into space. The Americans showed an interest, and he founded SpaceX.

He was always open to new experiences, and hired qualified specialists to develop designs for a solar city, a high-speed transportation system, and a non-profit company to research artificial intelligence. Those are now in process.

## Efficiency and a Good Sense of Organization

Millionaires always practice self-discipline. They have the unique ability to cast aside or postpone their own feelings and desires to relax in favor of getting a task done. They always create plans to monitor their behavior and schedules to meet their desired work-related outcomes.

For that, they are willing to sacrifice their own personal desires of the moment. They are stubborn and determined to achieve their particular goals. In fact, they are obsessive to the point that little distracts them. If you catch them on those days, and ask a question, sometimes they don't hear you. Once they arrive at a conclusion, they take action, and no one can stop them. They take what they need, if it's there for the taking.

## JEFF BEZOS

Jeff Bezos was the founder of Amazon.com. Initially, it was a website at which books were sold to the American public. Bezos started his business in his garage.

He was notorious for his organizational skills which he deliberately developed in his previous job at a hedge fund company. That kind of work called for close attention to detail. Because of that quality, he was often called a "micromanager," and exercised that trait at Amazon. Because of that prowess, he kept Amazon within the proper bounds of legal ethics. His organizational expertise served him well. When he sold his shares in Amazon, they were worth a market value of $62 billion.

## Extroversion and Energy

Millionaires are outgoing people, although there have been some exceptions to that. They are inundated by self-generated positive feelings and are optimistic even to the point of foolishness. These people thrive in the company of others, but always respect other people. They elicit the opinions of others by asking a lot of questions and showing a genuine curiosity about other people. They make others feel good about themselves. Howard Schultz, the CEO of *Starbucks*, often arrives at one of his shops and fraternizes with the customers. Millionaires learn a lot from others, and recognize that all relationships are two-way streets. Millionaires will tend to be talkative, but try to maintain a balance – something they often find difficult but rewarding. In the beginning, the millionaire-to-be may be perceived as domineering and attention-seeking. Most millionaires of any standing have learned to modify that domineering attitude. A less domineering approach tends to open up others to sharing good ideas. A good idea doesn't mind who has it.

---

## DOLLY PARTON

Dolly Parton's career in country music has gone on for 53 years and continues to this day. She is extremely energetic and never stops moving. She and her family were initially very poor. As a child, Dolly disciplined herself to reach out to others and was always a friendly person. Anyone who has attended her performances can attest to that fact.

Her love was and always will be country music. She began her career as a songwriter, which is not a highly visible field. As she wanted to make herself known publically, she started to perform nationally. She also realized that performers need to have control of their work. So, she educated herself in business practices and produced albums under her own brand.

---

### Competitiveness and Dynamism

Millionaires are always competitive, but that is relegated to situations that are within their fields of expertise. They may verbally strike out against another in certain circumstances when they perceive a real threat to their business. It is a shortcoming. A millionaire believes his or her project is their "baby," and they will defend it with every ounce of strength they can muster.

Millionaires are dynamos. They are extremely active both cognitively and physically. Their energy is overwhelming. If you think a millionaire is someone who sits on a luxurious tropical beach sipping Mint Juleps every afternoon, banish that thought. The Mint Juleps may last an hour at best. If they are on a beach, millionaires have their laptops on their laps, and cell phones in their hands. They will be there until the tide comes in and their lounge chairs start to float.

---

## LEONARDO DEL VECCHIO

Leonardo came from an extremely poor Italian family. He still speaks very little English, but that never dissuaded him from moving ahead. He first worked as an apprentice in the metalworking business, which served as a basis for the inauguration of his own eyeglass designs. He founded the eyewear company, Luxottica, which he set up as a limited liability company. His company faced stiff competition from Essilor, and Johnson & Johnson.

Luxottica lost a great deal of money due to competition from Essilor. It was quickly weakening. That is when he stepped in to reduce that competition, and after four long years, negotiated a merger with Essilor. DelVecchio was a dealmaker.

---

### Self-Assuredness and Stress

That seems to be contradictory, because it would seem that a truly self-assured person has less stress. Millionaires, on the other hand, are caught in a battle between true self-assuredness and vulnerability to stress. They focus upon goals, and feel increasing stress until they achieve them. That is part of the game. As they become more experienced, they become more relaxed. The first success a millionaire achieves is a pivotal milestone toward becoming more balanced. However, even so, the stress levels of millionaires still tend to be high. In this high-paced world, that has become commonplace. But the reward is much sweeter at the end.

## BILL GATES

In 1976, Bill Gates faced many hardships on his road to success. When he developed his nascent technology for MITS, others cloned his work. He then battled for his rights under copyright law, and was eventually successful. Afterwards, he and IBM formed a partnership. When they had differences, however, he created the DOS system to be used with his new product and spun it off to become Microsoft.

In 1980, he had a chance to partner with IBM. The only requirement was that he develop an operating system for them. Considering that a new and potentially lucrative job depended upon his ability to perform is a stress-inducing situation. Rather than flee from this, Gates worked day and night to fulfill their requirement. After much time and effort, he did come through and created the PC DOS system. That was the precursor of Windows.

Throughout his career, he had to fight for control of his copyrights, and had to defend his products against the onslaught of competitors. Often, he felt like he was surrounded by assassins. Bill Gates was a master at dealing with very stressful events.

## Risk-Taking

There is an old saying: "Noting ventured; nothing gained." Risk-taking is often viewed as a negative concept. Sometimes, that is ingrained during childhood. Sometimes societies are litigious, and worry that every playground accident will result in a lawsuit. Children hear that, and it only serves to reinforce their negative connotations about taking risks.

Adults carry that hang-up from childhood. Most people are also very sensitive to criticism, so they avoid trying something new and different for fear they will lose the esteem of others. They become afraid others will "laugh at them."

Million dollar companies feel differently. Cabbage Patch Kids come with "adoption certificates." How funny does that sound? Yet the Cabbage Patch Kids were a top-selling phenomenon, and every child wanted one.

In terms of business, you always take a risk with every new design, new plan, or new design. Sometimes people laugh. Sometimes the projects aren't successful. That is to be expected. But sometimes they are. That is the nature of risk.

As you go through the various millionaire profiles listed in this chapter, remember that every one of them failed at one time or another. Risk did not discourage them. A failure is a clarion call to modify, reroute, or develop a new plan of action. Just that, and nothing more.

Taking risks also demonstrates to the world that these up-and-coming millionaires-to-be are here to stay. They refuse to retire into their closets. Risk-taking is a show of confidence, and helps them gain attention. No one gets anywhere in life by "playing it safe." That is static. Without making a move, every person would be just one of the millions of other people and never reach their full potential. Everyone would be a member of the nameless "masses."

By attempting well-thought out risks, millionaires have learned to overcome those creeping fears of failure. The failure experience is nothing new to them.

# RONNIE M.

Ronnie was a cop in a heavily populated city. He was a strong and good cop. He knew the people on the streets, and the local businesses. One business in town was a theater in which noted entertainers and rock stars often appeared. He knew the owner as well, since he was often in that area.

Besides his work on the streets, Ronnie had a particular talent for maintaining the computers in the police station where he worked. He also could repair their communication devices. He liked to tinker and developed that skill on his own. Eventually, he was put in charge of all the police radios.

When the police department upgraded their equipment, Ronnie was also put in charge of maintaining the new equipment as well. He also asked if he could have the older devices. Having no use for them, the police captain readily agreed. Ron dreamed of starting up his own security company after his retirement from the force.

When he got his pension, Ronnie and his wife moved to a suburban neighborhood. Life was good there, but Ronnie wasn't ready to stop working and "live happily ever after."

Although he had enough from his pension to live comfortably, he took the risk of starting his own security firm with money set aside from his pension. Because he knew the owner of the theater in the city where he had worked, he contacted him with a proposal. Ronnie indicated he could provide inexpensive security for the entertainers, who were often mobbed by fans. In addition, the audiences sometimes got out of control at times. So, Ronnie guaranteed that he could manage them as well, and provide security using his own communication systems for his team.

The concept went over well, and his services were successful.

Soon, the word got out, and performers and entertainment companies hired his firm regularly. He then expanded his business through advertising and marketing.

Today, his security firm tours the world with famous rock stars and celebrities. His firm is one of the largest security firms in the entertainment industry today, and he is a millionaire.
Where does he live? In a suburban town in a typical middle-class neighborhood.

## Personal Frugality

Frugality consists of wise spending habits. Many millionaires practice this. In their study, Thomas Stanley and William Danko interviewed over ten millionaires and noted that most of them lived frugal lives. Many used that technique to gather sufficient capital to invest in their own businesses. Frugality brings with it a sense of resourcefulness, and the financial ability to get specialized training in a professional career.

# LI KA-SHING

Li Ka-shing was forced to quit school in China at age 12, after his father died. He had to support his family.

As a young man, Li Ka-shing worked as a salesman and later on in manufacturing. He learned about the plastics industry while working at a plastics factory. Curious about the possibilities of using color to expand the uses of plastics in decoration, he invested in his own plastics plant. When there, he developed plastic flowers that looked true-to life.

Because he was always a thrifty man, he retooled his manufacturing company to sell plastic flowers at low cost. A foreign buyer placed a substantially large order, and was extremely impressed with the quality of the product. Eventually, Ka-shing was the largest provider of plastic flowers and made his first fortune selling them in Asia.

Ka-shing is still known for his no-frills lifestyle. He wears simple black shoes and an inexpensive Seiko watch.

## Passion – Obsession Cycle

Millionaires are preoccupied with their major field of endeavor. In the beginning, it encompasses their minds. Everything is looked upon as a means to promote their personal interest. Those interests first arrive as casual hobbies or ideas. Eventually, they become pursuits which they examine thoroughly, research, and investigate. As those interests grow, millionaires analyze them for their potential money-making opportunities. Once they recognize that there is a monetary advantage to starting businesses related to those pursuits, they become very passionate about them. Goals are formulated. They gather the tools and information needed to attain those goals. They are attached intellectually and emotionally to their passions and then to the products or services that stem from them. They feel those interests will bring them personal fulfillment, success, and wealth. If they are frustrated in attaining their goal, they will develop tenable alternatives. Millionaires will always remove obstacles from their paths one by one, and often painfully.

---

# JUDI DENCH

Judi Dench loved to act. It was her passion. She embraced it as an expression of herself. She has done that all her life. She has starred in everything from Shakespearian plays to sci fi films. Even when her movies were flops at the box office, she would not quit. Acting was her lifetime passion.

In 2014, Judi Dench said: "I'm tired of being told I'm too old to try something. I should be able to decide for myself if I can't do things and not have someone tell me I'll forget my lines or I'll fall on the set." Her decriers were wrong. The following year, she starred in live performances, given nightly for two solid weeks. She also starred in two more movies that same year. The following year in 2016, she appeared in another role. In 2017, she appeared in yet another film.

---

## The Narrow Line between Obsession and Neurosis

Once the person moves from passion to obsession with their goals, irritability and extreme impatience may result. Obsessive people are difficult to work for and to live with. While millionaire personality types usually temper their tendencies to become dominant, obsession can threaten that success. The obsessive millionaire types usually take absolutely no offense when their staffs complain. It is the goal and the goal alone that gives them meaning. Their world moves faster and faster, and their actions sometimes lag the speed of cognition. They are not perfect, and can sometimes lapse into rather eccentric behaviors.

Whenever the success they feel reaches a level of significance, an existential fear sets in. Sometimes they feel that they will lose control because their success has resulted in something far greater than they had first thought possible. It becomes what some have termed a "fear of success." That is the danger point, because it can destroy what they have created. Many entertainers, for example, have turned to drugs and alcohol – all because they are afraid they cannot handle the work that accompanies success. That can happen to anybody.

Only those who have self-control and engage in socialization while they are on the way up will stop short of this. Successful millionaires quickly learn the difference between obsession and passion. The others embark on a path of self-destruction.

## Passion, Obsession, and Greed

Once a person or company permits obsession to evolve into greed, ethics may be cast aside for the sake of the "almighty dollar." That can happen on a small scale or a large scale. No one nor any company gets away with it forever. Bernie Madoff, cited earlier, is a prime example of this. He had great abilities as a financial broker, but became obsessed with his first string of successes. Not long after, he buckled under the temptation of greed and developed a scandalous Ponzi scheme.

> **Another costly example of greed:**
> In 2014, GM had to recall over 8 million cars due to a faulty ignition switch. It was determined by the courts that this was due to an uncorrected problem that started on the engineering level and was permitted to continue by management. It was reported in the court records that there was a "business decision to ignore the defect." That decision resulted in over 100 deaths.
>
> GM lost a fortune. Many key personnel were fired, and victims' families still cry out for criminal prosecution.

# 2

---

# THE PERSONAL TRAITS
# OF A MILLIONAIRE

Check off the characteristics that apply to you:

___ A. I am an extrovert.

___ B. I am always open to new ideas.

___ C. I am a quick study.

___ D. I formulate goals and work until I achieve them.

___ E. I am optimistic.

___ F. I am a leader.

___ G. I hate wasting time.

___ H. I have trouble being patient with stupid people.

___ I. My thoughts tend to race rapidly.

___ J. I am always making plans.

___ K. Sometimes I interrupt other people.

___ L. I am a logical person.

___ M. I do not consider myself a genius.

___ N. I am very rooted in reality.

___O. I am competitive.

___P. I am very stressful at times.


Millionaires tend to manifest those traits, even some of the less desirable ones. They usually have a perennial struggle with those negative characteristics. They may have more money than you, but they are subject to the same human foibles you have.

You will also note that you have many of the traits millionaires display. No doubt, you have noticed that some traits on the list are negative. Millionaires are also human; they are no different than the average person. Of course, there are some traits you don't have and might like to work on developing them.

**Ways to Compensate for Your Missing Qualities:**

A. **"I am an extrovert."**

If you aren't an extrovert, there is a way to compensate for that. Develop an idea for a product, a service, or a business. You probably already have one brewing in your mind. When you must socialize, talk about that idea. You will find it extremely easy to get fired up about it. You can be an extrovert when you talk about something that inspires you. Seek out the opinions of others regarding your idea. The additional benefit to that is the fact that you may meet other people who have knowledge and skills in your area of interest.

B. **"I am always open to new ideas."**

If you are not open to new ideas and hear a wild and crazy idea from someone, try visualizing it in action. Your visualization will be privately amusing to you. Now try to modify it in your mind and enhance it with your own touches and additions based upon your current skills and knowledge. Something that sounds bizarre and crazy may very well be the foundation of a new venture.

**Real-Life Example:**
Kaitlin lived in a very poor fishing town. She had very little money, but wanted to start making money – lots of it. Because of her poverty, she didn't want to spend her money buying expensive curtains, but needed something for her windows. One day, as she walked along the shore where the fishermen had their boats docked, she spotted a lot of discarded old fish nets. She asked the fisherman why they were discarded. He replied: "We are not allowed to use the old-fashioned netting anymore…the fishing regulations now call for nets designed to allow for the escape of turtles and other types of inedible sea animals."
"May I have some?"
The fisherman then said she could have all she wanted. "What are you going to do with those?" he asked.
"Make curtains out of them," she replied.

The fisherman thought she was *crazy.*

Kaitlin took them home, bleached them, cut them to size, and draped them decoratively on her windows. They looked beautiful. After that, she decided to collect more and more. Then she carefully cut the nets down to standard window sizes, dyed some of them, and put them into plastic bags with photos of her own window treatments. She then rented a table at a local flea market. Kaitlin sold so many of them that she was able to invest more and more into the product. Today, Kaitlin runs 120 craft shows and is a millionaire! All that money came from a crazy idea.

C. **"I am a quick study."**
    If you take a very long time to learn, read…read…read. Your reading can be in any genre that appeals to you. You can even learn a lot from fictional characters.

D. **"I formulate goals and work until I achieve them."**
    Most people don't have difficulty formulating goals and objectives. However, many are pommeled with one goal…then another…then another to the point where it is no longer possible to work towards only one goal. Set very short-

term and simple goals for yourself. For example, straighten out your desk drawers. Force yourself to continue until you are finished. That will slow down your thinking process. You can develop more exercises like this for yourself.

### E. "I am optimistic."

If you aren't an optimistic person, that will take quite a bit of work. First of all, visualize a cartoon picture of a silly-looking sourpuss in your mind. That's you! Think about the cartoon every time you get crabby. That cartoon will help you laugh at yourself a bit. Secondly, force yourself to smile. It is hard to be pessimistic when you're smiling. Thirdly, when you experience a pessimistic thought, exaggerate it. If you just lost some money, picture yourself losing more and more and more to the point where it gets ridiculous.

### F. "I am a leader."

If you don't feel you are a leader, you can still develop that trait. Socialize with just a few close friends, and you will notice that you actually can be quite expressive. You can also widen that small circle of close friends by adding one or two more people. You can also take a course in public speaking. That is a terrific morale booster.

### G. "I hate wasting time."

If you tend to waste time, the solution is clear. If you tend to goof off, start by cleaning an area of your house. Or do a little something you *hate* doing. Very quickly, you will come up with a more productive idea for becoming active.
The one thing to keep in mind is the fact that you need to rest sometimes. That will give you much needed time to think and to relax. You are human.

### H. "I have trouble being patient with stupid people."

If you tend to be impatient with stupidity, you will need to remind yourself that stupid people also deserve respect. That is something you would need in a new business pursuit. There is stupidity everywhere, even among those who make a lot of money. Have you ever seen those Dilbert cartoons?

"The illiteracy today is appalling. His stock
certificate says: '50 CHAIRS'!"

## I. "My thoughts tend to race rapidly."

Millionaires have a tendency to experience an onslaught of ideas. They have learned to focus on one or two of them. If other ideas seem good to them, they delegate others to work on them. Some people have difficulty getting their thoughts together. They need the kind of stimulation that actually may come from reading ads, as surprising as that sounds. Also, reading business magazines helps stimulate ideas and thoughts.

## J. "I am always making plans."

Wealthy people make a lot of plans. Sometimes they can get lost in a labyrinthine network of plans. They often find that they need to narrow their focus and set up a simpler system. Simplicity is usually a much better approach for business planning. Sometimes infographics and flow charts are like street maps of the world.

## K. "Sometimes I interrupt other people."

Rich people tend to be somewhat domineering, but the most successful of them have disciplined themselves to allow for the free expression of their employees and partners. The successful have learned that they should never, ever "believe their own publicity."

**L. "I am a logical person."**

If you feel you are not logical, it is because you feel someone has said that about you. Never, ever accept that as a fact. You are hard-wired to be logical, although your skills may not be strong. You are attempting to start a business or develop some means of becoming wealthy. Focus on clearing up the mental fog, and the process will be easier.

---

## EXERCISE IN MILLIONAIRE-STYLE LOGIC

This is not your usual exercise in logical reasoning, like you learned in school. It is an exercise in *selling* through the use of logic.

Watch a few commercials and record them. The purpose of virtually all of them is to sell a product or service.

1. Record a commercial and replay it.
2. Note the outcome of the commercial and write it down.
3. Replay the commercial again.
4. Listen to the first couple of statements. Pause. Write down a few keywords to remind yourself of those statements.
5. Listen to the next couple of statements. Again, pause and write down these keywords.
6. Continue until the commercial ends.
7. Go back to your notes.
8. Notice how the advertiser led you down a path that logically led to the decision to buy what they were selling.
9. Notice how sensible they made it sound.
10. Notice how they featured low price.
11. **Notice how a potential buyer is left with no other logical option but to purchase from them.

---

**M. "I do not consider myself a genius."**

Many, many millionaires are not geniuses. The ability to earn money is independent of IQ – these two factors have been proven to have no correlation whatsoever. Of course, a high

IQ does not mean you cannot be a millionaire.

**N. "I am rooted in reality."**

If you are very innovative and creative, there may be a tendency to fantasize a great deal. That is terrific in developing ideas for a business or such that can make you a lot of money. However, you are what is called an **"Idea Person."** What you need most is a business partner who is a **"Practical Person."** This should be someone who is well-trained in business practices and very skillful in promotional techniques. Above all, it needs to be someone you trust implicitly. Before embarking on such a partnership, remain absolutely open to the other. Let the other take the lead in setting up a viable business plan. Refrain from getting carried away or producing more and more ideas. Far too many partnerships dissolve because the "Idea Person" becomes too dominant. He or she then holds the more practical partner back. Unfortunately, some practical people have often taken their partners' ideas and successfully marketed them. Those occurrences are usually NOT betrayals; they happen because the practical people become totally frustrated. So, follow your practical partner's suggestions carefully, and contribute sparingly. The other will ask you for more input. Practical people recognize and admire the value of creativity.

**O. "I am competitive"**

If you are shy about competition, focus on your prime objective: to make a million dollars. Then focus upon accomplishing one small success. Once you have had one small success, do not congratulate yourself over and over again. Be successful again. Keep focusing on the final outcome. Do *that* all the time. Try to achieve more and more small successes. If you keep this up, those little successes will ignite a fire within you that cannot be extinguished.

*Refrain from listening to negative feedback in the beginning. Once you have developed a thick skin, negative feedback can be taken in a selective and positive way. The tendency to avoid competition is really masked fear.

**P.** **"I am very stressful at times."**

Millionaires are very prone to stress. All of life has some degree of stress. If you are heading towards making a fortune, you will be more stressful than most, and will need to find proper relaxation techniques to help you.

However, if you happen to be too relaxed and lazy, you have failed to take up the gauntlet. Arthur would never have become a king if he slept by the rock that held the sword meant for him.

# 3

------------

# FINDING YOUR NICHE
# USING PERSONALITY STYLES

Millionaires all have different personality styles depending upon their inborn gifts, their personal characteristics, their upbringing, and their environment. Because of these differences, you will find millionaires in many different fields. Those fields match their personality styles. All people can make a lot of money, but that usually happens in an area of interest that is in keeping with their own personality.

Millionaires are aware that wealth does not flow directly from their occupations or career choices. It has to do with the traits they manifest, as well as their personalities, experience, skills, and interests.

Expert writers often say: "Write about what you know." If you set up your new business based upon what you already know, you are halfway there. Too many people underestimate their own value in terms of skill and experience. Through all your adult years, certainly you have learned something. You may tend to take those skills for granted. You have also been born with personal characteristics that can serve you well in a future business. Perhaps you are charming. Perhaps you are an amusing person. A lot of business lacks humor; however, that is an extremely desirable personal skill. If you were the kind of child who often started up jokes in the classroom, you were probably corrected by the teacher for causing a ruckus. If you have lost that trait, recover it. That is the key to socialization and the first stage of developing charisma. Like those students of the past, people will gather around you – anxious to hear what else you have to contribute. That's a good start for a motivational lecture for your employees or team members.

Most likely, you are already working. During the course of that work, you have noted particular aspects of your work which were of significant interest to you. You have also discovered areas of your job or in your company which you disliked intensely. Regardless of whether or not you liked your work, you have developed skills that can serve you well in future endeavors.

John Holland of John Hopkins University developed a list of personality types that suited particular occupational interests. Millionaires have different personality types. There is no such thing as a "wealth" personality style. Millionaires have personality styles like everybody else, including you. They start out in different occupations. Success depends upon what one does with their natural personality, as well as their skills, and experience. The list of occupational examples given is not a complete one, but the descriptions will give you an idea of what your most successful niche will be.

*Your niche lies in areas that suit your personality style, experience, current skill sets, and interests. You can sell products and services more easily in those areas. Once you have had a decent amount of success, you will have the confidence to break into new fields. John F. and Dolly Parton from the earlier chapters did that. John moved into commercial real estate and Dolly moved into being a record producer.

**Exercise:** Look at the descriptions of the personality types developed by Holland and classify yourself in one or two. Then refer to examples of areas that may be more successful for you to pursue. This list does not list all the fields in which you can be most successful.

| Personality Types | Fields |
|---|---|
| **Doers/Manual**<br>Stable, use tools and machines, are manual, and think concretely | Car mechanics, contractors, gardeners and landscapers, physical fitness trainers, nature guides |
| **Investigators/Thinkers**<br>Analytical, methodical, rational, technical, problem-solvers | Accountants, computer Software writers, technical writers, web developers, financial advisors |
| **Creators/Expressive**<br>Intuitive, nonconforming, original, verbal, literary, communication | Graphic artists, musicians, screenwriters, models, business trainers, counselors, chefs, writers |
| **Social/Interactive**<br>Empathetic, helpful, friendly, tactful, diplomatic, generous | Counselors, teachers, educational administrators, customer service |
| **Persuaders/Enterprising**<br>Ambitious, assertive, confident, persuasive, dominant | Public speakers, salespeople, lawyers, marketers, promoters |
| **Organizers/Conventional**<br>Conscientious, logical, orderly, detail-oriented, accurate | Tax advisors, order clerks, business administrators, engineers, wedding planners, efficiency experts |

There are two exercise examples in this chapter for setting up a side business. The first is a general example of the application of your work experience alone to find a possible niche for you. You may already have one in mind.

The second exercise is an example of how you might adopt not only your work experience, but also your personality style and personal skills toward creating a new venture for yourself.

## General Example Based on Work Experience Alone:

**Scenario:** Jayne worked at an auto body shop. During the course of her work, she was asked to assist the mechanics in finding parts for the older cars in their shop. Jayne was very organized, and detail-oriented (Organizer personality style). She also knew a number of parts suppliers while she worked at the shop as an order clerk. Her goal was to become a self-employed supplier of hard-to-find classic car parts for the auto restoration business. Classic auto restoration is a very lucrative business.

| Step One: | Step Two: |
|---|---|
| Jayne saved a little seed money to start. The goal of her new business was to find needed parts and and sell them to the various classic car restoration shops in her area. She reviewed her own files at work and made a list of the most common suppliers. She also sought out other possible suppliers from eBay and discussion groups. She then scoured the internet to locate more classic car restoration shops (her potential customers). She gathered together copies of the trade magazines she had at the shop, and subscribed to more. She contacted all the possible sellers and told them her plans. Many were interested. She then knew there was a lot of interest in her service. | Jayne then used her seed money to take out ads in all the popular trade magazines and on the internet. She also printed up some shipping labels with her logo, and mailed them to the sellers, who were instructed to use those labels and mail the parts directly to her customers. When orders came in, she located the parts needed. She had the sellers quote the price and she agreed to pay them. She then added some extra money for herself and quoted the higher figure to her buyers. Once the buyers sent her the money, she had her sellers ship the parts directly to the customers using her label. Only a packing slip was included in the shipment. That technique is called drop shipping. |

There are other businesses you could set up based on your personality style, skills, and interests. If you are in the field of education, you could take on a partner to develop an app for your teaching program and sell it to teachers and schools. If you are of the persuasive type, you might set up a guest speaker's bureau for companies who want motivational speakers.

If you want to make money selling a product or service, it is crucial that:

1. You really like the product or service yourself.
   Have you ever heard a car salesman say: "I have that car myself?" That reeks of deception, doesn't it?
2. You have quite a bit knowledge about it, even if it is self-taught. Use the product; explore all its possibilities and experiment with it.
3. Its use fits your own personality style.
   If you hate wearing makeup, don't try to sell it.
4. You have some knowledge as to whether or not it is of general interest to others.
   That takes a little bit of parlor conversation. Sometimes, it may even include hiring a few students to stand in a shopping mall and asking folks for their opinions. That is called a "market survey." It is especially important if you are introducing a new product.
5. You know some potential buyers of your product or service.
   Make up a few prototypes of your new product and see if you can sell them at a kiosk in a shopping mall or in a cart at a street market. If you are interested in developing a new service instead, send out some emails asking potential customers for feedback.
6. You know people who might help you make important business contacts.
   That takes a bit of networking. Mentors and advisors also can help and will be discussed in a later chapter.
7. You have a general idea about how to actually market your service or product.
   Use your visual imagination. Picture how it would look in the

store. Picture how it might look on your upcoming website. Scribble down some ideas as to what you might say about the product or service. Figure out ways you might advertise it by looking at other ads. Listen to TV commercials, and ask yourself about how those vendors market their products. Then try to outdo them.

Do not buy some unknown person's "miracle" plan for setting up a business. Do not buy "courses" offered by people you've never heard of before. Otherwise, you might be victimized by a scam. Start a new business armed with knowledge, not dreams. Your new business is to be uniquely *yours* – not one that is designed and laid out by someone else with a template or formula.

## Predicting the Trends

Young people are the biggest spenders. A huge number of advertisers cater their ads to the younger generations. They deliberately exaggerate the power of self-image in achieving success, and the young tend to be vulnerable to that appeal. However, if you look more closely, you will discover that there are many, many wealthy people – both young and old – who are NOT good-looking at all, do not wear the latest fashions, and do not fall for the latest gimmicks. Those folks, too, represent potential buyers. An example of this is the real estate market. Realtors market their housing to various generations. The best marketing trend is one that appeals to more than one generation. In terms of determining the trends, it helps to observe grass roots movements, economic conditions, and the geopolitics of all age groups.

Technology occupies a highly respected spot. Today, hundreds of thousands can develop their own apps. Health and exercise is worth examining. Manufacturing and real estate is on the rise in certain countries. Cultural events, vacation travel and reading are also on the rise. In some countries, education is emphasized. The food industry is risky, but many can make their fortunes in that. The organic food industry is strong and can give rise to related industries like gardening, and the development of environmentally-friendly pesticides.

## Your Skills, Experience, and Interests for Choosing Your Niche

A lot of people underestimate their skills because they take them for granted. You could have a nice smile and friendly telephone manner. You could be quick with figures. You could be a very social person. Even minor skills can be important in creating a new pursuit. Work experience is priceless, even if you hate your current job. Because of your work experience, you have more knowledge about an industry or service that you would never have had, if you weren't working. Every experience you have had in life – not necessarily related to your job – has given you a new skill. For example, perhaps you used to take nature walks and learned about the flora and the fauna of a forest. Perhaps you dance very well or you like to build fancy dollhouses. Maybe you know a lot about fly fishing. All experience counts, and the sum total of it makes you who you are. Think about your personality type, your work experience, and your skills. Then draw up a plan like the one shown below for a possible side venture you might like to pursue.

**Scenario:** Betsy works for a wholesale fabric company in the bookkeeping department. Some of her skills are her own; others were learned. She gained all her work experience on the job, and some from other jobs she has held in the past.

On the next page is a list submitted by Betsy. It contains the essential ingredients for starting her own enterprise:

| Skills | Work Experience | Interests |
|---|---|---|
| • Has a pleasant phone voice | • Maintains current database at work | • Gourmet coffee |
| • Has great arithmetic skills | • Handles accounts payable and accounts receivable | • Scrapbooking |
| • Loves to chat with people | • Has some knowledge of fabrics because that is the company business | • Planning social events |
| • Is able to learn new computer apps quickly | • Handles company ordering | • Traveling |
| • Is a good decorator | • Answers the telephone | • Dancing |
| • Bakes quite well | • Knows how to handle customer complaints | |
| • Is great in organizing social events | • Has knowledge of shipping and loading | |
| • Popular in the social media | • Has knowledge of packaging | |
| • Is a coupon collector | | |
| • Is very persuasive | | |
| • Is very orderly | | |
| • Is a speed reader | | |
| • Knows how to budget | | |
| • Does tax forms for friends and relatives | | |

Looking across the board, one can see that Betsy has the skills to handle many of the tasks involved in creating a new pursuit. One of her strongest is her ability to budget and handle figures. She also has a ready-made initial client base due to her popularity and activity in social media circles. She can always expand that skill into other forms of communication.

Many people don't realize that their casual skills are real assets in business. For example, Betsy is good on the phone. She is also persuasive, which means she can sell.

Taking into account her personal skills, her interests, and her work experience, Betsy could be very successful in becoming a wedding planner. She could also hire herself out to a more elite population by becoming a party planner for more wealthy people. Her pleasant telephone voice will come in very handy. She only has to investigate the usual fees others would charge for such services. As her business becomes larger, she could hire and train other assistants.

Because she is social, Betsy could hire herself out to small cruise lines as a social director. She is friendly and outgoing. She also dances (one of her other interests). What's more, she likes traveling. Her business holds a lot of promise for expansion.

Although she loves dancing, her other skills and work experience might not be much of a contribution toward making her successful as a self-employed dancer. Yes, she could open up a dance studio, but lacks the professional connections necessary to make it very far in the entertainment sphere or appear on stage. That road would be longer and harder to travel.

Now, if she wanted to, she could open up a vendor's booth selling gourmet coffees with recipes for purchasers to make *Starbucks*-like coffees as home. She likes to decorate, so her booth could be carefully designed to attract customers and draw the largest crowds. Betsy has familiarity from her work as to how to deal with wholesale vendors from whom to buy her products. Because she is persuasive, she can gain just a few more skills for negotiating with providers for the best deals. Her little booth can eventually become a little shop, and then expand into a chain of specialized shops once she supplements it with some of her baked goodies – another one of her skills. She could sell her coffee cheaper than *Starbucks*. Someday, if she continues to succeed, *Starbucks* might even buy her out. Do you see how it can grow?

As for her love of scrapbooking, she might find that this is truly a hobby and might not become a lucrative business.

Now it's your turn. Writing up this entire task will help you remember it. On a sheet of paper or in a word processing program, make up a list made up of three columns like the one below. Write down all your skills, including casual ones. List the skills you have learned from your job, and your interests. Then highlight the skills, experience, and fields of interest that can be connected to create a successful business. Too many overlook their minor skills and learned work experiences.

| Skills | Work Experience | Interests |
| --- | --- | --- |
| | | |

It will help you a great deal to copy this diagram and actually do it up as if it is a real business. As you work on it, you will notice that you will be making important revisions and refinements. There are pitfalls you might notice if you really focus on doing a good job with this exercise. There are also all kinds of opportunities that might stumble upon you.

# 4

---

# FALL IN LOVE WITH
# YOUR PRODUCTS

From the previous chapter, you have identified your personality type, analyzed the values of your innate and acquired skills, your work experience, and your general interests. Once you link your personality style with your skills, interests, and experience, you will have the ability to successfully run your own business. With hard work, you can make it grow into a million-dollar success.

In the course of your life, you may come across some products or services that really, really interests you. One clerk who worked for a company that sold vacuum cleaners and household appliances was asked to write up blogs about the products. At first, she detested the project. However, as she wrote the blogs, she produced extremely persuasive pieces and eventually became very excited about the products herself. When she talked to her friends about her work, she was so enthusiastic about the products, that her friends started buying them from her company. Not only was she excited about the products, but she discovered that she could become a great saleswoman. And she never dreamed she could do that.

You also have miscellaneous personal interests as well. Read everything you can about your personal interests. Expand your knowledge. For example, if your interest is organic gardening, and you love planting and cultivating, you are a "Doer," who prefers manually directed tasks. Perhaps you are a bookkeeper by trade, and that has given you some abilities to understanding monetary concerns. You also have an awareness of profit/loss from your observations. That knowledge alone will give you some fundamentals for creating a budget and measuring profits.

To bolster your interest in gardening, for example, you should read everything you can about the field. You could also learn ancillary material like the use of organic pesticides, the medicinal properties of certain species of edible plants and herbs, the use of green vegetables for low-fat diets. Earnest pursuit of that simple interest in gardening can go into a variety of different directions:

- Selling plants in your own retail business or nursery
- Setting up a florist shop and perhaps expanding it in the future
- Publishing and selling recipe books using organic vegetables which can expand into selling this genre of written material to larger markets
- Selling herbs or herb extracts on the internet for medicinal uses
- Publishing and selling weight-loss cookbooks
- Selling organic vegetables at farm markets, or perhaps opening your own farmer's markets in the future
- Reselling of organic pesticides supplied by a wholesaler, along with your own printed material on usage
- Reselling of organic cleaners created by some wholesale businesses

## Specialization

Once you have stirred up those fires of excitement within you, and opened up your own nascent business, you might like to narrow your focus into one aspect of your field of interest. That will put you into a better position by reducing the competition. A person with an interest in car repair, for example, might consider specializing in trucks only. That narrows the field quite a bit. Many general repair shops cannot handle truck repair, so the local competition will be less. He or she could sell at a discount. In the beginning, business expenses could be much lower than larger shops, if the location is wisely chosen. Insurance costs would be much lower than a dealership that has to insure an entire fleet of trucks as well as the lot they occupy. On the side, the new entrepreneur could rent out trucks or sell tires as well.

Think about the kind of people who could mentor you in the pursuit of an interest. These would be people who are experienced in your field of interest. They also need to be people you can trust. If you think you might need a partner, sweep across your memory for people:

- Who can perform tasks that you are weak in, for example, bookkeeping or data processing
- Who you can trust implicitly

**Exercise:**
This exercise aims at learning to expand your thinking.

For the exercise, note the interests and hobbies listed in the left column. In the right column, write down the number of businesses that might grow from exploring those interests more deeply and the kind of businesses that can be born from serious pursuit of those interests. Get expansive about it and also include a possible million-dollar business that can grow from a simple interest.
The first one is done for you as an example.

| Interests and Hobbies | Possible Businesses |
|---|---|
| 1. Physical fitness<br>2. Playing the trumpet<br>3. Cooking<br>4. Beekeeping<br>5. Blacksmithing<br>6. Amateur car racing<br>7. Dolls<br>8. Animals and pets<br>9. Photography | 1. Becoming a certified physical trainer<br>2. Teaching local classes<br>3. Inventing a new form of group exercise and appearing on a local TV show<br>4. Opening up your own gym |

# 5

---

# YOUR BUSINESS PLAN

## Goal-Setting

How everybody hates that topic! It doesn't sound like fun, does it? It is work, but it is the skeletal framework which will support your initial attempts. Taking into consideration your skills, experience, and interests, a process of elimination must occur. No one can do everything. Certain final objectives will only require some of your skills and experience. No one can run helter-skelter into many different directions at the same time. For example, "Betsy" in the earlier diagram could go into the making and selling of gourmet coffees. If that isn't a raging success in the first couple of months, she should not abandon it in favor of becoming a wedding or party planner. Your new project deserves much more time and devoted attention to make it work.

Just recently there was a new show introduced in the US. The network bought 16 episodes of it, but cancelled the show after the first two episodes. They claimed it was because of "poor ratings." Now, how could they possibly make that determination after just two episodes? They failed to give it a ghost of a chance. It is rare that anything will be a raging success immediately. The first Star Trek series got off to a slow start as well. Later on, it became a billion-dollar series with many sequels and spin-off shows.

Goal-setting is **decision time.** In order to arrive at success, it is necessary to set up an action plan. According to Branden: "A goal without an action plan is a daydream." In the following exercise, there are sections for concrete actions. That way, there is no confusion as to what to do next. Furthermore, there is no excuse not to continue in your road to success.

# GOAL

| | |
|---|---|
| **Product Research** | Trends?<br>Customer base?<br>Can it be lucrative? |

| | |
|---|---|
| **Marketing and Promotion Research** | Methods?<br>General costs?<br>Venue? |

| | |
|---|---|
| **Preliminary Actions 1***<br><br>*Make no monetary commitments at this time | Locate and contact list of possible marketers and their specific fees:<br>• _____<br>• _____<br>• _____<br>• _____<br>• _____ |

| | |
|---|---|
| **Providers***<br><br>*Make no monetary commitments at this time | Requirements on your part?<br>Specific costs?<br>Methods of delivery?<br>Vetting the providers.<br>Insurance needed for you and/or them? |

| | Locate and contact list of possible providers and their |
|---|---|
| **Preliminary Actions 2\*** | fees: |
| | ● _____ |
| *Make no monetary commitments at this time | ● _____ |
| | ● _____ |
| | ● _____ |

| | Locate and contact list of possible places to rent (if needed) and determine rental |
|---|---|
| **Location of Your Business\*** | fees: |
| | ● _____ |
| *Make no monetary commitments at this time | ● _____ |
| | ● _____ |
| | ● _____ |
| | ● _____ |

If your new project is going to be service-oriented, you may need to set up a different kind of diagram to suit your needs. However, the above will give you an idea of how much planning you may need for an independent start-up business.

In a later chapter, legal suggestions will be presented for setting up three different types of business structures: the **sole proprietorship, the Limited Liability Corporation (LLC), and the Chapter S Corporation.**

**Note:** Foreign companies can set up businesses in the US using the Limited Liability Corporation (LLC) status.

## A Simple Organizational Timetable

It may be a pain in the neck to do this, but it is absolutely crucial to keep track of the routine tasks like keeping up your in-house inventory, paying your invoices on time, issuing new blogs, updating your website, keeping up with social media campaigns, paying your sales taxes on time, keeping up with your office supplies, and the like. Who wants to look at their invoices and see that late fees have been added on? It is most often not because you don't have the money; it is because you "got busy," and failed to heed a proper schedule of designating time on a bi-weekly basis for paying bills. This can happen to both a small company and a large company. One time, a very large insurance company bought another company, and "got so busy" that they failed to process customer payments in a timely manner, resulting in customer penalties. Their agents were inundated with calls from thousands of customers complaining that it took the company nearly a month to post their payments to their accounts. It was the company's fault that the customers were charged penalty fees. Afterwards, they had to go back and correct every single transaction that they themselves had fouled up. That cost them months and months of unnecessary time redoing what should have never happened in the first place. It also cost them a lot of money, as they had to pay their employees overtime to rectify the errors.

In the beginning, you should be starting with a small business. That alone will make it easier to develop a fail-safe system. This helps you to be thrifty and avoid unnecessary aggravation, time, and money if you plan well.

## Outsourcing

Yours is a small business to start, and it would be wise to outsource some of your more tedious duties to independent contractors and to job brokers on the internet. This way, you can devote your time to selling your product or service. Sub-contractors are skillful at keeping up with your sales campaigns through blogging, doing up press releases, developing ads and brochures, executing email campaigns, writing up material for the various social media outlets, updating material on LinkedIn, Google+, Facebook, Twitter, and the like. A simple Google search will yield thousands of subcontractors you can hire. Be sure to do a price and quality comparison. Not every subcontractor will perform as you might like. Have them revise their work if need be. As they learn your products, they will be able to meet your standards.


## Mentors

The following is a long segment, because mentoring is one of the most valuable resources you can tap into when you take your first steps. Mentors are like open vaults of information – information you cannot find on the internet.

Everyone needs a helping hand, especially in a new business. While you may know your service or products and have a tenable business plan, there will be aspects about running a new business you are not aware of. Mentors know all the secrets of the trade. They will know things not written in books or taught in courses.

Although there are mentoring programs widely advertised on the internet, it is not recommended that you seek services from those. They will be much more expensive than finding your own mentor. The interactive programs on the internet will not be sufficient. Something very magical is lost that way. While they may be fine for conducting a business transaction, they limp when it comes to genuine human contact. Computer screens create barriers. You could really benefit from a personal mentor whom you can talk to face-to-face.

While you were investigating your new business, no doubt you came across similar companies and independent contractors working in your field. Select a mentor from one of them. Of course, pick someone who is nearby. Independent contractors usually have web sites that will tell you a little bit about themselves and where they are located. Brush up on your telephone skills, determine what department to call in a company to locate someone you might hire to be a mentor. If you are calling the particular department of a company – for example, the sales people or the buyers – chat a bit. Don't seek out someone of executive status; choose someone who is lower on the totem pole, so to speak. Find out how many years of experience the person has. Plainly and simply state your needs.

People generally get very little personal recognition. The person you have chosen will be complimented at your unique request. Like you, they too need the esteem of others. Most mentors that are privately recruited are very generous in their advice. Some even bring their own literature and references that you can utilize.

Indicate you want private instruction. As indicated earlier, face-to-face mentoring sessions are best.

You will need to pay the person, so make a reasonable offer. Have them visit you a number of times, or you could travel to see them instead. State your objectives. Ask that the person bring in samples of their products or brochures. People feel good when you show a sincere interest in their accomplishments.

### Benita the Cartoonist

*Benita only had a little training in cartooning and art, but knew she had very good skills, most of which were self-taught. When she embarked on a side business in cartooning, she hired a mentor. He was a teacher at an art and cartooning school not too far from her. He arrived with samples of his work, a set of special ink pens, a computer software program, catalogs, and a lot of professional materials. She wasn't aware of such products. He taught her not only how to execute and present single-panel cartoons, but also comic strips. In addition, he was skilled in realistic art, and taught her techniques for that. Every time he came, he gave her "homework" projects and critiqued them upon his next session.*
*The two of them got along famously.*

*After she had more sessions with him, he brought her a list of computer links directing her to lists of possible markets for her to sell her work.*
*True mentors are not threatened by a student's skills. They are strongly secure and confident in themselves, so the sharing of such information is easy for them.*
*After their sessions were over, Benita could always call for help or to ask questions.*
*Mentors consider their students "protégés," and are proud of their student's*

*accomplishments.*

*Benita's cartoons are licensed worldwide today, and her realistic work appears in major publications. Her mentor, who once worked for Archie comics, now has a comic book line of his own. He also teaches in several universities.*

## Courses

If you need to take a few courses, avoid the hyped-up ones offered by some firms on the internet. The most frugal investment is to take some adult education courses offered at your local community college. Even some high schools offer courses. Perhaps you have a firm business plan, but realize that you are weak in computer skills. Perhaps you are good with some manual trades, but need a more disciplined presentation to avoid common pitfalls. Of course, you can take on a partner to do that for you, but it is essential that you have some basic knowledge of the craft yourself.

Maybe there is, in your field, a certification requirement. There are usually services for that on the internet. You may need to renew your business licenses as well, if it is required. Those certificates on the wall of your office impress contacts and customers alike, much like diplomas impress patients in doctors' offices.

# 6

---

# THE MILLIONAIRE-MINDED MONETARY LIFESTYLE

The majority of millionaires own their own businesses. In the US, 66 percent of them do. When you are starting out, it is essential that you have total control. Later on, you can set up a limited liability corporation or a fully formed corporation. Those will be explored later in this book.

All millionaires create a cushion of capital for their businesses. These are for the times when the economy is sluggish. Below is some advice for building your capital cushion.

### MILLIONAIRE-MINDED MONETARY LIFESTYLE

1. Live frugally. Dress for success, and get only a couple of expensive suits or outfits for high-level occasions.

2. Ask your banker about the various kinds of accounts they have available, and the requirements of each. You may be able to save on bank fees with another type of account.

3. Set up auto-pay systems for important bills like your mortgage. Keep a sufficient amount of money in your accounts consistently.

4. Check all of your regular accounts for billing errors. You might find that you are being charged for phone calls you haven't made, for instance. That is more frequent than most folks realize.

5. Pay off credit cards in full each month if you can. Credit card companies charge very high interest rates. If you cannot pay your bills in their entirety, work like heck until you can reach that level. Some credit card companies have "cash back" programs that can be applied to cut down your balances.

6. Never be late paying your bills. If you do lapse, call the credit card companies and try talking your way out of late fees. If you have a good record, they may let you slide. They want your business.

7. Keep your cell phone expenses to a minimum. There are some cell phone companies that charge lower rates.

8. Avoid subscribing to software as much as possible. If you terminate a subscriber service, contact your credit card company or bank and tell them in advance not to permit any more of those charges to be honored. Software companies have a notorious way of "overlooking" that.

9. Never, never pay termination fees to a company unless you signed a contract to that effect. Without a mutually signed contract stipulating that, it isn't legal.

10. Avoid dining out as much as possible. When you do go out, choose an inexpensive place.

11. When you cook, try cooking as much as you can "from scratch." Prepared meals and processed foods tend to be more expensive (and not that healthy either).

12. Grocery shop in the inexpensive stores.

13. Shop at farmers' markets.

14. If you are a good worker, ask for a reasonable raise.

15. Never buy "gimmicky" items that you don't actually need.

16. Do not buy from a telephone solicitor. You have no way of vetting the company or researching it. Select a product, and then you can call them. You are in the driver's seat.

17. Never get involved with "causes." "Cause people" are those who protest on a political or social issue which they consider unjust. While their cause may very well be a just one, you will consume a lot of time demonstrating, distributing paperwork, planning, meeting with groups, and the like. That is unpaid work. After you are a millionaire, *then* pursue the issues you feel are important. Many millionaires have set up foundations and charities later on in their careers.

**Warning:** You want to buy less expensive goods, but be careful. Cheap things do not always deliver value. There are many, many products on the market that are sub-standard. Also, on the big ticket items, it is better to buy for reliability. They may cost more, but will last longer.

# GROWING CAPITAL TO START
# YOUR BUSINESS

Most millionaires were self-employed at a side business when they started. For that, you will need a certain amount of capital. So, even before you start, invest.

All people can invest – even the poorest of people. A simple money-market fund or your bank pays only a pitiful amount of interest. The best kind of asset in which to invest are **Appreciating Assets.** That means that the investments increase in value over time. They consist of index funds, stocks, stock funds, bonds, mutual funds, and Exchange-traded Funds (ETFs). There are other more sophisticated instruments like hedge funds and derivatives, but those are best handled by very clever and experienced money managers who specialize in those products.

Warren Buffet's first investments were long-term ones. Likewise, you should plan that way. Over the course of a number of years, your investments can grow significantly. As you no doubt know, there is always some risk involved. Thus, it is important to watch trends. Today, technological products tend to do well, but you need to watch carefully, as many of the newer companies fail.

## Tax Awareness

Educate yourself on the taxes that will be due because you will be earning money from your investments. Research on the internet, and ask a lot of questions. Learn about the allowable deductions. If you have even a small side business, there are a number of them permitted. Some can even occasionally be applied to personal use, such as telephone or computer usage. If you own a house, and use a part of it for your side business, that is deductible. Postage and shipping expenses for your business also present opportunities for deductions.

## Best for Beginners: ETFs and Stock Funds

ETFs, or Exchange-traded funds, are collections of bonds, stocks, and/or commodities. Stock funds are families of stocks similar to ETFs, but only contain stocks. They are managed by companies who trade the stocks and bonds in the fund depending upon market conditions. Those managers are specifically hired to locate the most profitable new money products and engage in selling others within the portfolio. You can easily get access to the values of these funds on the internet or from your broker if you select a private brokerage. You might also choose to sign up with a discount brokerage.

The best ETFs are usually those who are doing something very similar to what they had been doing five or even ten years ago. So, check their histories on the internet. "Fixed Income" funds are ETFs that contain some bonds. That will help allay some of the volatility of stocks.

Stock funds tend to vary somewhat as industries shift with the economic times. Read some of the financial reports publicly available to spot trends, and try to buy at the bottom. That is a guess, of course, but the stock market and funds are somewhat of a gamble. Keep in mind that most heavy investments are made by middle-aged people. Therefore, what may be the latest rage among teenagers and the 20-somethings may not last long.

---

*Warning*

An IPO or Initial Public Offering occurs when new companies first start issuing stocks. Usually those are not accessible to the ordinary investor right away. If you see an ad advertising a new company and encouraging you to buy its stock, **beware.**

---

*Warning*

Perhaps you will be successful, and want to sell that fund or stock for a profit and buy something else. If you do that very often, that is called "churning," and will cost you a lot of money in the long run. Remember, each time you sell and buy, there are fees involved. Some investment outfits advertise that they have no fees, but there are other kinds of fees they charge for their services. So, **beware.**

---

Sometimes you will see a depreciation in the value of your package. Don't panic. That's very common. Hold off and watch the progress over a longer period of time.

## Stocks

Although they tend to be less stable than bond funds and stock funds, individual stocks are nice start-up investment learning tools. Select companies that have a long tradition. Carbonated beverages like Coca-Cola, for example, might be good. However, check the history of any potential purchase, look for the low and high of the year, and buy when it is at or close to its yearly low. Buy into the kind of company any idiot could run. Failures are more often due to poor management than to market fluctuations.

---

*Warning*
Stocks tend to be "emotional." When there are geopolitical changes in the world, a lot of stocks fall. Usually that is just a temporary setback. So don't panic. That's due to institutional trades that are automatically done by computer. Often, right after a downfall, other institutional trades rush in and stocks start selling again. Just watch your portfolio carefully and read the stock reports for those of concern.

---

## Dividends

Invest in products that pay dividends. A dividend is the interest a company will pay you, based upon the amount of money you have invested. If a fund pays you 5% interest an investment of $200, that will become $210 by the end of the month. The best practice is to permit the dividends to remain in the fund you select, so they can be reinvested. Some funds pay monthly; others just pay quarterly.

As your dividends increase, you have the option of placing the dividends from some of your investments into your cash account, rather than reinvesting them. You will need easily accessible cash from time to time.

## Compound Interest

According to Albert Einstein, compound interest is "the greatest mathematical discovery of all time." If you left your $210 in your fund, you would have $231.52 by the end of three months.

Dividends are based on this compound interest. It is like "interest paid upon interest."

## WHAT TO AVOID

Unless you are a very experienced investor, avoid getting involved in monetary vehicles such as hedge funds, commodities, futures, and engaging in short sales. That's akin to gambling.

## Index Funds

These are very long term passive investments. If you can hold them for years, your profits will soar. They are extremely reliable monetary instruments. An index fund is a "bucket" of stocks, bonds, and other funds. In order to be one of the money instruments included in an index, the stock or bond must have a proven track record, and be considered an excellent product for increase in revenue over time. The best known stock and bond indices are the Standard and Poor 500, the DJ Wilshire 5000, the MSCI FAFE (non-US stocks), the Russell 200 index, and Barclays Capital Aggregate Bond Index. Check to see which stocks and/or bonds have dividends. It isn't entirely necessary that there are dividends (some of them are very small), but your risk is minimal because it is spread over a large area. Index funds outperform the stock market. After taxes, they can yield around 8% or more annually.

No commission is charged on index funds. The managers of these funds consult the ratings on investment research companies such as Morningstar.

# 7

---

# DEMOGRAPHICS AND STATISTICS OF MILLIONAIRES

Are millionaires in a separate bracket all their own? Were they brought up by wealthy parents?

The answer is a resounding NO.

Contrary to the prevailing opinion, millionaires today were brought up under all socioeconomic circumstances. Most were raised in a middle-class household. Only a small amount of them were raised in wealthy households. Their educational level tends to reflect that of the general population. Most millionaires are self-made millionaires. The one feature that does seem to separate them from the general population is the number of hours they work per week.

This chapter delineates the demographics of millionaires in terms of background, budgeting and general expense patterns, as well as fields or industries in which most of them work.

# SOCIOECONOMIC STATUS PRIOR
# TO REACHING MILLIONAIRE STATUS

| Socioeconomic Group | Percent |
| --- | --- |
| Poor | 19% |
| Middle class | 48% |
| Wealthy | 33% |

| Type | Percent |
| --- | --- |
| Self-made millionaires | 80% |
| Other | 20% |

*80% of millionaires own their own business*

| Type | Percent |
| --- | --- |
| Inherited startup money | 58% |
| Secured through loans or self-financed | 42% |

# EDUCATION

| Type | Percent |
|---|---|
| Law Degrees | 8% |
| Medical Degrees | 6% |
| PhDs | 6% |
| MS | 18% |
| BS | 20% |
| No college degree | 20% |

# WORKING BEHAVIOR

| | |
|---|---|
| Work 5-6 days per week* | 80% |
| Retired | 20% |

*Of those who are still working, they put in 50 hours per week on average

# BUDGET AND EXPENSES*

| | |
|---|---|
| Personal Expenditures | 41% |
| Investments | 15% |
| Taxes | 38%* |
| Other | 6% |

*USA figure

As indicated in Chapter 1, **The Traits of Millionaires**, most millionaires are notoriously frugal. Clothing expenses generally ran about 5% of their annual net income. Car and related car expenses (e.g. insurance, gas, maintenance) ran about 12% of their annual net income. That would include other family cars, like those for their children of driving age. Insurance expenses are more difficult to calculate, as many companies carry some of those expenses. In terms of life insurance, some of those companies run as sole proprietorships and LLCs frequently were named as one of the beneficiaries. That is because the policy owners do not want the companies to fail when the founder or founders die. Separate contracts are sometimes drawn up to protect spouses/children who do not work for the businesses. (e.g. "Buy-sell" agreements)

## Some Notable Facts about Taxes and the Wealthy[*]

Although many believe that the "rich" only pay 4% in taxes, this is an unfounded rumor. It is true, however, that many executives have some of their expenses paid by their companies within legal limits. For example, many companies provide cars and related car expenses to their top administrators, including the owners, of course. Other expenses may be assumed by the companies such as certain insurance policies. Owners and other top executives can deduct expenses for dinners and luncheons for their clients, company meetings, or affairs.

Some retired millionaires and billionaires run foundations. They may be salaried through the foundations, but the salaries have to be modest, in keeping with the provisions of a non-profit organization.

*Information only applies to the US*

On the following table, note that as many as 12.3% - 12.4% of millionaires drive cars that are between three and six+ years old.

# CAR BUYING HABITS OF MILLIONAIRES

| | |
|---|---|
| Current Year | 23.5% |
| 1 Year-Old | 22.8% |
| 2 Year-Old | 16.1% |
| Three-Year-Old | 12.4% |
| Four Year Old | 6.3% |
| Five Year Old | 6.6% |
| Six+ Years Old | 12.3% |

## MOST POPULAR PERSONAL
## CAR BRANDS FOR MILLIONAIRES

| Rank | Make | Percent Owned |
|---|---|---|
| 1. | Ford | 9.4% |
| 2. | Cadillac | 8.8% |
| 3. | Lincoln | 7.8% |
| 4. | Jeep | 6.4% |
| 5. | Lexus | 6.4% |
| 6. | Mercedes | 6.4% |
| 7. | Toyota | 6.2% |

*As for vehicle model, millionaires tend to buy the most reliable and long-lasting vehicle for all-purpose use. That is usually the top-of-the-line model for that make of vehicle.

## TOP INDUSTRIES THAT PRODUCE WEALTH WORLDWIDE

| Rank | Industry |
|:---:|:---:|
| 1. | Investments |
| 2. | Fashion and Retail |
| 3. | Real Estate |
| 4. | Diversified |
| 5. | Food and Beverage |
| 6. | Technology |
| 7. | Manufacturing |
| 8. | Energy |
| 9. | Finance |
| 10. | Media |

## TOP INDUSTRIES THAT PRODUCE WEALTH IN THE USA

| Rank | Industry |
|:---:|:---:|
| 1. | Investments |
| 2. | Technology |
| 3. | Media |
| 4. | Energy |
| 5. | Food and Beverage |

The data above is heavily skewed toward the investment sector. Millionaires are notorious for their ability to save and invest money. Therefore, there are many more opportunities open to service them in that area.

TOP INDUSTRIES THAT PRODUCE WEALTH IN CANADA, CENTRAL AMERICA, SOUTH AMERICA, AND THE ISLANDS

| Rank | Industry |
| --- | --- |
| 1. | Finance |
| 2. | Fashion and Retail |
| 3. | Food and Beverage |
| 4. | Diversified |
| 5. | Media |

TOP INDUSTRIES THAT PRODUCE WEALTH IN ASIA-PACIFIC

| Rank | Industry |
| --- | --- |
| 1. | Real Estate |
| 2. | Diversified |
| 3. | Manufacturing |
| 4. | Fashion and Retail |
| 5. | Technology |

# TOP INDUSTRIES THAT PRODUCE WEALTH IN EUROPE

| Rank | Industry |
|:---:|:---:|
| 1. | Fashion and Retail |
| 2. | Investments |
| 3. | Metals and Mining |
| 4. | Energy |
| 5. | Food and Beverage |

# TOP INDUSTRIES THAT PRODUCE WEALTH IN MIDDLE EAST AND AFRICA

| Rank | Industry |
|:---:|:---:|
| 1. | Diversified |
| 2. | Construction and Engineering |
| 3. | Finance |
| 4. | Metals and Mining |
| 5. | Food and Beverage |

The above data is skewed, considering geopolitical situations. For example, in some countries, certain industries (oil-energy sector, for instance) are government-owned.

# 8

---

# MISTAKES NOT TO MAKE

1. **Start-up Is Too Soon**
   Before embarking on a business of your own, save up enough capital to fund it. For example, suppose you want to go into the business of buying foreclosed or inexpensive homes, refurbishing them, and offering them for resale. Be sure you have the money to pay for the improvements, as they may cost more than you anticipated. You will also need some extra capital to repair unforeseen problems that may arise. Suppose it was discovered that some of the electrical wiring was aluminum. According to the law in most states, that has to be replaced before the house can be resold.

2. **Initial Investment Too Much or Not Enough**
   Imagine you have a terrific plan for business and are in need of an office. Be very frugal in choosing your first office. One unwise fellow set up an accounting office in the southeastern US. Instead of finding something in a less prestigious neighborhood, he rented out a large office. He was so proud of his plans, that he even added a bar to his conference room. The office had the finest carpeting and the most exquisite furnishings in the executive office, a conference room, and a waiting room. He was out of business in two years. Likewise, if you are setting up a professional office, secure enough capital to set up your office in an area of your town or city that houses other such offices. Putting it into a strip mall will not attract much business. Location is extremely important. With regards to location, check out the neighborhood around your desired location first. You don't need 5 other companies right around you that are direct competitors.

3. **The Rent**

When you set up your own business, you might be able to start out in your garage. However, as your business grows, you will need to rent space. There are ways to rent at a reasonable rate if you negotiate. After all, rent goes up annually in most cases. You might consider negotiating a 3-year rental contract at the same amount. Landlords always look for long-term tenants. If you obtain a 3-year agreement, the rent for others in your building may go up and – after two years – you may actually be paying less than they are. After three years, you will know whether or not your business can grow. Should you be so lucky as to have it expand, squeeze into your current quarters as long as you can. You can always find an ancillary space to supplement the influx of business, until you can risk moving to a larger space.

4. **Weak Product or Service**

It would be best if you sell a service or product with which you have some familiarity. If you are only familiar with one aspect of your potential business, it might be wise to partner with someone who can handle the other aspects of it. For example, suppose you are skilled in vitamin supplements and you want to sell them. Would anybody buy them? What if vitamin supplements aren't selling well? Always check out the trends first. Always read the reviews on similar products.

What if you buy a wholesale item for resale that might turn out to be defective? Have you tried it out yourself? Have you read the reviews? Have you researched the popularity of the item?

5. **Believing in Your Own Publicity**

You may very well develop a very popular product or service. Your friends laud you. Your reviewers love it. They all admire you, and expect much more from you. Your company name starts gaining recognition. Your promoters and marketers rave about you and your talents. If you read and reread their favorable press releases, your own marketing literature, and ads and actually believe them, you're in trouble. Advertisers always exaggerate, and some even lie a little. That is no time to feel that you are now "King of the World." Never let your ego become greater than your common sense.

6. **Underestimating the Buying Public**

Consumers are quite astute. They always evaluate a new purchase in terms of quality and price, among other things. Suppose you have a terrific everyday item and are selling it at a tremendous discount. However, you charge a huge shipping and handling fee to avoid any loss. Customers will notice. Your sales will be few, and you will have complaints. Suppose you run out of a brand, and substitute another. More complaints (and returns) will roll in and sales will inevitably suffer.

"Did we get any feedback from that customer yet?"

7. **Failure to Handle Complaints**

Always treat your customers with great courtesy, even if they are unreasonable. The phone and the social networks are very powerful, and your reputation as a company can plummet because of disgruntled customers. Read your feedback. If a lot of complaints are similar, it is time to take action.

## 8. Failure to Maintain/Correct/Modify Your Services or Products

Flowing from the above scenario is the issue of maintenance and repair. Losses can be very gradual and sneak up on you if you fail to note that your customers are the most important part of your business. Yes, your office needs to look somewhat prestigious and you do need to pay increasing insurance costs. However, the last place you should look upon to cut costs is your service or product. Failure in that category could wipe you out.

> *"Yikes!" the electrician shouted when he saw the first box. It had no cover and all the wires looked like psychotic spaghetti. "Was your other electrician spastic?" he asked.*
>
> *Later there was another shout from the attic. "Aaaack! No wonder half of your outlets don't work. Didn't that guy know that every wire has two ends??"*
>
> *$2000 later, Sam had working electricity. He realized that it is better to spend money in the right places than have your house burn down.*

## 9. Lack of Wisdom regarding Loans

Companies sometimes take out loans too soon – that is, when the business is in its nascent stages. Also, they may take on loans that are much too large, or it is at a time when the interest rates are very high. Become familiar with standard practices when dealing with banks. Never take out a loan because you "expect" that your business will increase in profitability beyond what it is making now. Do what you can to conserve and cut costs wherever you can until your business actually *is* larger and really does need a loan.

## 10. Failure to Budget Carefully

When you have laid out all your plans, be extremely conservative in your spending. There will be times when you will have more than enough, and are turning a good profit. Keep putting some money aside…just in case. Watch carefully, because every business runs in cycles. There will be slow times, and you will still need to pay your rent and your vendors.

Please...continue with your meeting. Don't mind me...
I'm with another company!"

## 11. Raising Your Prices Too Quickly

No matter what your product or service is, you will always have competition. They will watch you carefully. When you raise your prices, they will offer discounts. Your customers watch too. Don't count on customer loyalty, because they consider price increases betrayal. If you raise prices quickly, they will leave as rapidly as a stampede of wild mustangs. Guarantee improvements and upgrades for your products before raising prices. And, by all means, make those improvements and do them right. That is how you garner customer loyalty.

## 12. The Logo

It's OK to get excited about your new business venture. However, many people spend a lot of time and money on designing their logos. Yes, one's logo is important, but it is not as if you are creating a baby. The same is true for the font you decide to use. It is the name of the product or service that is the most important.

## 13. Failure to Trademark and Copyright

Never downplay your ability to produce something of value. Your logo should be trademarked along with any mascot(s) you may use. It is not expensive if you trademark it inside your own country. Worldwide trademarks are very costly. You can do that later if need be.

Your website name can also be trademarked. Someday you may want to sell it, and trademarked web sites can sometimes attract big buyers, particularly if it has a catchy name. One entrepreneur, for instance, paid $500 to trademark her web site name, and sold it for $65,000 eight years later.

If you have original text material, get it copyrighted. Through the auspices of Berne Convention in 1948, most countries in the world are bound to abide by the conventions of copyright law.

Images you own can also be copyrighted. Of course, if you are not the original artist, you need to have a contract with the artists to that effect. Images may also be licensed, which is an added source of income for you.

## 14. Investment in a Business You Can't Control
You need to have the space and the tools necessary to start a business. Suppose you jump into a business and discover that you cannot afford to provide all the services that purchasers might require. For example, let's say you have a couple of tow trucks that you plan to use for delivering vehicles for small companies. What if those companies want the vehicles delivered hundreds of miles away? You wouldn't have the time nor the personnel to do it in a reasonable length of time.

## 15. Underestimating the Costs of Advertising and Promotion
Printing brochures and business cards is very inexpensive. However, you will need to look into internet advertising as well. Some of the deals they offer seem inexpensive, but the wording in their offers is very tricky. Agreeing to a contract like those may yield exorbitant fees. If you sign any agreements, be sure you can terminate anytime. No fee should be charged for termination unless the contracts are signed by both parties.

You will also need to promote your business. If you have the expertise, do it yourself. If not, check any internet firm on the "Whois" database to determine how long they have been in business. You do not need a teen working at the task from his bedroom. You need a company with experience. Note: Make many press releases and hire blog writers.

# 9

---

# FRIENDLY FIRE

## The Steady Stream of Self-Appointed Advisors

Watch out! Once you toss around your ideas for a new enterprise and get it into the initial planning stages, your friends and relatives will offer all kinds of advice – from the sublime to the ridiculous. Some of that is genuine, but there will always be some envy involved. Among your friends and relatives, many may want to "jump aboard" and act as partners. This will require some tact, as you do not want to start out with ten people! What's more, how many of them would be willing to invest in your project? How many of them have the vision you have? How many actually have the time to spend in order to bring your project to fruition?

Remember, too, that friends and family may want to support you. They may tell you that your idea sounds terrific. They just want you to feel good. However, they themselves may not even buy your service or product at all.

Be very, very careful about who you choose to share your ideas with. Seek out people who are neutral and objective, but do not give away your idea too readily. They may very well steal it. Caution is the keyword here.

## The Services You Hire

Naturally you will need to reach out and hire some companies and individuals to assist you. Never, never say you are a "Start Up Business." That attracts vultures. Can you picture every marketing outfit barraging your inbox with offers? Can you picture every freelancer approaching you? Because you are naïve, protect yourself from the onslaught of companies and people who may be far less than adequate.

It is going to be your company. You are the boss. So, you should make is a concerted effort to find the right people first and solicit a few of them whom you feel may have sufficient expertise to help. You will need to propose a budgetary figure to them. Avoid quoting a figure that is much too low. Otherwise, the best person for the job may be so insulted that you won't hear from them at all. Your budget should be a reasonable one. That will take a little research.


## Your "Friends"

This has happened more than once, sadly enough. When you first set up your business – watch out! A dear friend of yours or an acquaintance may come out with their new business too. It will not be unlike yours. There are a number of reasons for this. Many are emotional. Some of your "friends" may think that your idea is a great one, and they want to make a profit for themselves as well. Others may be jealous. Others may feel insulted that you haven't partnered with them. Yet others may be angry they didn't think of the idea first, or perhaps they want to "get back at you."

In case that occurs, your best option is graciousness. Simply congratulate them. If they did that for purely emotional reasons, they most likely will not be successful. After all, their emotional mindset was negative. No one starts a business and works hard to develop a viable business plan, conducts market research, and sets up an organizational structure fueled by negativity. Your new "competitor" will quickly lose his or her steam. Once the negative emotions have subsided, they will lose interest.

In the "grown-up" businesses of millionaires, you will see copycat businesses arise, but that isn't fueled emotionally. That proceeds from the spirit of competition. If their new businesses offer more quality or are marketed more widely than yours, they may actually overtake you. Note that *Facebook* outpaced *My Space* in ratings and popularity even though *My Space* was first on the scene. Some of that was due to quality;

some of that was due to marketability; and some was due to financing. That happens. If you cannot afford to buy them out, you may need to look for an alternative.

When you go into business, you are painting a target on your back. That is reality. Avoid emotionality over the fact that others will try to take your place. Grow a thick skin. Even if you change the nature of your business, you **will succeed.**

*Note:* Never borrow money from friends when you start up. What if you have to change the direction of your business? What if you made an error and have to change your product offerings due to market conditions? What if you have to move to a new location? Changes are sometimes inevitable in the beginning, and that will cost you more money. You do not want to be placed in the embarrassing position of not being able to pay the money back to your friends in a timely manner.

# 10

---

# CURIOSITY OUTPERFORMS MOTIVATION

## Curiosity as a Means to Stimulate Motivation

> By the time she was 32-years old, Kimberly could operate a forklift and a drill press, run equipment in an industrial laundry, operate huge scrubbers and polishers used in institutions, do simple auto repairs, and the like. Today, she runs a private vocational school.
> What was her profession when she started? Teaching and counseling! During summers she worked as an office temp.

How did she learn all those skills? She was curious. Through her work experiences, she developed a curiosity about the settings in which she worked. When she was a teacher, she became curious about the janitor's heavy-duty equipment and learned how to operate some. When she was office temp at various companies, she sometimes strayed into the shops and plants themselves asking the employees to show her how the equipment worked. No one ever seemed to show interest in the entry-level employees in those places, so they happily let her watch. Of course, her presence there was against the rules, but she usually got away with it at the various companies because she could play "Sally the dunce." Her curiosity about manufacturing and her work experience in teaching and counseling set off a startup business in running a vocational school. She can also spin that off into a network of schools.

---

### The Curiosity Story of a Millionaire

Chameleon Cold-Brew generated $9 million in US sales in 2015. By 2024, when it is sold worldwide, analysts predict that it will yield $116 billion in sales. How was Chris Campbell, one of the company's founders motivated? By simple curiosity. It started in a coffee shop in Austin, Texas. Chris simply asked questions about the delicious coffee he was drinking.

He then investigated finding his own coffee beans and flavorings and experimented until he came up with an excellent coffee drink.

A project such as that requires a lot of hard-nose work in goal-setting and action steps to lead to the final outcome. He and his partner started out frugally – by renting a refrigerator in a commercial kitchen. Chris and his wife used a portion of their savings to start the business rolling.

---

Chameleon Cold-Brew generated $9 million in US sales in 2015. By 2024, when it is sold worldwide, analysts predict that it will yield $116 billion in sales. How was Chris Campbell, one of the company's founders motivated? By simple curiosity. It started in a coffee shop in Austin, Texas. Chris simply asked questions.

Nurturing the curiosity of the child within you takes the bite out of going through a series of tedious intellectual tactics and mental gymnastics. Ultimately, it increases your motivation to become a millionaire.

Everyone tends to take the easier road. When anyone has to step out of his or her comfort zone, stress occurs. Confrontation with new and challenging experiences send out signals to your brain carried by what are called "neurotransmitters." Those, in turn, set off hormonal and bodily reactions. The one that operates in stress is epinephrine. That stimulates the adrenal glands to produce adrenaline and the "fight-flight" syndrome ensues. The easy solution to this arousal of stress is "flight" – that is, to run away from a challenge. In view of motivation and the achievement of success, to flee is totally nonproductive. This is what is operative when it comes to the risk-taking trait. Millionaires demonstrate that trait overwhelmingly. They do not engage in "flight" from a challenge; they "fight" to take it on.

Through the vehicle of curiosity, one can often bypass the stress of the "fight-flight" syndrome discussed above and achieve great successes.

Einstein once said: "I have no special talents. I am only passionately *curious.*"


## Curiosity Produces Charismatic Leaders

Some people are most interested in becoming wealthy by rising in their corporations. Many of them are also millionaires as they rise to the top of the pay scale and can even share in the ownership of a company. Curiosity is a user-friendly way of fueling one's own motivation. The curious employee discovers more and more about the workings of an organization. The side effect of this can be self-transformational. One can actually become the kind of person who is capable of assuming such a leadership role. Young managers who engage in curiosity can attract the attention of superiors through the charm and likeability that flows from their curiosity. Upper management would look at a curious employee as someone who authentically shows an interest in the company above and beyond the humdrum 9-5 workday.

Curious managers learn a lot about their teams. They also draw to themselves innovative people like themselves. One's positivity about the future is boosted by that.

People gravitate toward team leaders who are interested in them and people will want to produce the best results for them. Those successes impress upper management.

## Curiosity and Risk Taking

Curiosity reduces fear when one practices it more and more. The result of curiosity motivates people to find out new things. Risks and fears become less threatening and that cultivates motivation. Curiosity can be a strong drive that inspires extraordinary risks. The rewards of curiosity are seen as a much more desirable prizes than the comfort of curling up into the fetal position of the status quo.

## Curiosity is as Vital as Intelligence

Tomas Chamorro-Premuzic, a professor of Business Psychology and CEO of Hogan Assessment Systems, has coined the term "Curiosity Quotient." In his article for the Harvard Business Review, he stated that: "CQ leads to high levels of intellectual investment." He says that the curious can deal with major management complexity much more easily than those who are not curious.

The curious live in a mindset of wonder and awe. They are innovative, and understand the value of good customer relations. They can create solutions while the person with a high IQ is lost in a forest of intellectualizations.

## Erica's Story

As an eight-year old, Erica stayed with her uncle for a week while her parents were away on vacation. Her uncle had a small business and he worked at it in his house. Erica was a curious child and asked him a lot of questions about the business, and listened to his replies. Instead of playing with the toys she had brought, she went into an adjoining room equipped with some pencils and a stack of white paper. She was busy for over an hour and a half. After she was finished 'playing,' she invited her uncle to see what she had created. She then showed him stacks of paper neatly piled. One pile was stacked with 'orders.' Another pile contained 'invoices.' Other piles were brochures, business cards, pretend cash, and the like.

Today, Erica manages a series of 20 stores.

# 11

---

# TAX ADVANTAGES OF SETTING UP YOUR OWN BUSINESS

## General Tax Advantages for US Citizens

### Customer Advantages for Non-US Companies in the USA

If you are a US citizen, you have to pay personal income taxes. Look at all that money you shell out in costs to run your own business like office expenses, computer expenses, advertising expenses, website expenses, etc. You cannot take those as deductibles on your regular IRS return. What if there was a way you could? Your tax burden would be much less. By setting up a sole proprietorship, such expenses are deductible. The same is true if you have partners (the Limited Liability Corporation-LLC). If you have a larger group of people involved in your business, you could set up a Chapter S Corporation.

If you a non-US citizen, you could set up an LLC in the USA, charge for products in American dollars, and increase your American customer base. Many potential American customers may hesitate if they feel they will be subject to fluctuations in the currency exchange. At least one of your partners needs to be a legal resident of the US, but not necessarily a citizen, in order to quality for status as an LLC.

### Sole Proprietorship

This is the appropriate set-up for someone working out of their house or out of a very small office. Protection is essential to prevent lawsuits.

No, you don't need an insurance policy in most cases unless you are in the professional field. Usually, the kind of protection you would need is nothing more than a standard policy for delivery and return of unwanted items. For a very small business, you would simply need to establish a system for return of goods if your customers are dissatisfied with your products or services. Keep impeccable records of the customer's purchases and maintain adequate records of your own. Your business records should be kept separately from your personal expenses and other income you may have.

If you offer a service, there are standard contracts available on the internet. *Important: use the simplest one possible that has nearly no penalties. Otherwise, you might scare off some individual customers. Be sure fees and deadlines are specified. It is good practice to ask for a reasonable deposit when working with private individuals. Have confidence in yourself! You have something to offer. Customers are impressed with that.

For a sole proprietorship in the US, report your business income on Schedule C. You are also entitled to a series of deductions for business expenses, as indicated on that form. For example, you might use your computer almost exclusively for your business. Therefore, any computer expenses may be deducted, including computer repair. If you use an accountant, he or she should be instructed to make the necessary deductions for depreciation. Other expenses are accounting and legal services, professional materials, marketing, advertising, and the like. Telephone expenses should always be included. If you use your car for business, that is deductible. If you take a client to dinner, the dinner is a deductible expense. You will have to pay self-employment taxes as a sole proprietor.

# For Partnerships and Non-US Citizens: The Limited Liability Corporation (LLC)

Without hiring a lawyer, there are ways to set up an LLC for yourself. Check the internet for references, but **be sure the sites are legitimate.** There are many small outfits around that are not knowledgeable, and will attempt to sell you a package you don't need.

The US government has official web sites for establishing Limited Liability Corporations, and other types of Corporation. It is helpful to look under the heading of the Small Business Administration.

LLCs are very popular, especially for small businesses for a variety of reasons. They do not have to file a lot of forms with the US government.

The biggest advantage in establishing an LLC is the fact that your liability is limited. If your business has the misfortune of being sued by a disgruntled customer and he or she is successful in the suit, a settlement is not levied on you personally. Your personal assets are exempt.

It is up to the members of the LLC as to what to take in terms of profits. One member who contributed 80% of the capital could take more profit than the partner who contributed 20%. During a slow period, a member can take a reduced amount of money in order to help the LLC survive. As a partner in the LLC, you would pay taxes on your business. If you hire people, most LLCs hire subcontractors who are responsible for their own taxes. Otherwise, they would have to remit employee taxes to the government. If you have a regular job elsewhere, taxes are computed differently. You do not have to file corporate reports. The LLC files taxes as a "C" corporation. The IRS has forms and instructions available for that.

**The "EIN"**

Some vendors and suppliers will sell products to you at *wholesale* prices only if you are a legitimate corporation with an Employer Identification Number (EIN). It gives you a better reputation. Wholesale suppliers are wary of buyers without the assurance that you are a business that can be trusted. With the EIN, you will be able to buy at a discount, and not have to pay up front. That gives you time to sell the products before you have to pay for them. Even if you don't live inside the USA, you will need the EIN if you want to do business inside the US with a US-based wholesaler. The IRS web site has forms for obtaining the EIN. It is simple.

**Chapter S Corporations**

If you have more partners/owners and employees, Chapter S corporations might be the way to go. Like the LLC, you would have liability protection. Income that goes out to its members is not taxable to the corporation. The members pay taxes on it. Corporations issue shares to its stockholders, who are the owners/members of the corporation. They can also issue more stocks and sell them to the public. (up to 100 shares) This would provide the corporation with added income. Tax filings occur annually.

More paperwork is involved in setting up a corporation and there will be need of quarterly reports of income/loss. Chapter S corporations are only open to permanent residents in the US and US citizens. It is recommended that folks in this category hire accountants with a CPA.

If a Chapter S corporation hires employees, it is expected to pay unemployment, disability, and other payroll taxes and remit that to the government. Corporations also need a Federal Tax ID Number (which is different from an EIN).

# 12

---

# OVERVIEW AND CONCLUSION

The greatest trait of a millionaire is the fact that he or she is happy in their field of work. They are in love with it.

That is what this book is all about. Achieving your dream of being:

1. Happy
2. Rich

In elucidating the traits of a millionaire, you have noticed that you, too, possess many of them. You have discovered that millionaires are not born in ivory towers. They worked hard and did their best. They weathered the storms that assaulted them and came out fighting.

Millionaires aren't born with some kind of "millionaire gene." They learned how to become millionaires, as you noted throughout this book. Even many, many heirs and heiresses have actually squandered their money. So, becoming a millionaire has nothing to do with that sort of luck. In fact, the parents of future millionaires insisted that their children work. Many even required their children to get entry-level jobs.

Some of today's millionaires failed in college. Some had to make many attempts to get into ivy league universities. Some never finished their studies. Others had to quit school because they became the sole support of their families. Yet others were raised in poverty.

The more you have read in this book, the more the millionaires seem to be just like you. They are human; they are flawed. They fail many times, but pick themselves up just like you do in life.

You were presented with some very practical tables that utilize all your personal skills, your work experience, and your interests that can result in the formation of a very lucrative business for yourself. This book contains practical guides you can use to set up your own business, including the raising of capital, and creating a viable business plan that suits *you*, and not someone else.

All of the recommendations in this book can be applied to climbing up the corporate ladder in your current job, rather than setting up your own business.

Ways and means of overcoming your shortcomings were suggested, keeping in mind always, that the culture of perfection promulgated in the world today is a myth.

The monetary mindset and practices of the millionaires were delineated, and should serve as techniques you should imitate. Their monetary practices made a lot of money for them. Thus, those same practices can make money for you.

Some pitfalls that will occur to those who are just starting out are exposed. Through that, you have learned how to avoid getting caught up in traps you haven't yet anticipated.

Instead of plowing through a lot of philosophical abstractions like "motivation" and the perennial "do not quit" quotations, this book has taken the much more realistic path.

The more tedious of obligations were explained thoroughly like securing an Employer Identification Number (EIN) and creating a business structure, the most common of which are Sole Proprietorships, Limited Liability Corporations (LLCs), and Chapter S Corporations. Tax implications and advantages of all of those types of business frameworks were likewise discussed.

All of the anecdotal examples given, whether they be about the well-known millionaires, the lesser-known millionaires, and the people on their way up, are ***true to life***.

It only remains for me to say now:
*May you become rich and famous!*

# ABOUT THE AUTHOR

Stefan Cain has spent the majority of his working career in numerous academic research positions, working on a wealth of psychological, societal and cultural topics. His research work and adept studies have been used to form the backbone of many popular titles available today, providing him with the experience and hunger to delve deeper into some avenues of thought.

Alongside his serious academic work, Stefan has been published in a number of prominent publications; filing news reports, features and insightful opinion pieces on myriad topics throughout his career. It was here, in this capacity as a journalist, that he first began to start writing about human behavior.

Made in the USA
Las Vegas, NV
05 November 2021